Daniella Monterroso

Explore THE U.S.A.

WEST VIRGINIA

Laura Pratt

LET'S READ
AV²
BY WEIGL™
ADDED VALUE • AUDIO VISUAL

Go to www.av2books.com, and enter this book's unique code.

BOOK CODE

U 5 1 2 1 7

AV² by Weigl brings you media enhanced books that support active learning.

AV² provides enriched content that supplements and complements this book. Weigl's AV² books strive to create inspired learning and engage young minds in a total learning experience.

Your AV² Media Enhanced books come alive with...

Audio
Listen to sections of the book read aloud.

Video
Watch informative video clips.

Embedded Weblinks
Gain additional information for research.

Try This!
Complete activities and hands-on experiments.

Key Words
Study vocabulary, and complete a matching word activity.

Quizzes
Test your knowledge.

Slide Show
View images and captions, and prepare a presentation.

... and much, much more!

Published by AV² by Weigl
350 5ᵗʰ Avenue, 59ᵗʰ Floor
New York, NY 10118
Website: www.av2books.com   www.weigl.com

Library of Congress Cataloging-in-Publication Data

Pratt, Laura.
  West Virginia / by Laura Pratt.
     p. cm. -- (Explore the U.S.A.)
  Includes bibliographical references and index.
  ISBN 978-1-61913-417-1 (hard cover : alk. paper)
  1. West Virginia--Juvenile literature. I. Title.
  F241.3.P73 2012
  975.4--dc23
                        2012016587

Printed in the United States of America in North Mankato, Minnesota
1 2 3 4 5 6 7 8 9 16 15 14 13 12

052012
WEP040512

Project Coordinator: Karen Durrie
Art Director: Terry Paulhus

Weigl acknowledges Getty Images as the primary image supplier for this title.

WEST VIRGINIA

Contents

3

This is West Virginia.
It is the Mountain State.
West Virginia is made
up of many mountains.

This is the shape of West Virginia. It is in the east part of the United States.

Where is West Virginia?

N
W E
S

Canada

United States

Pacific Ocean

Atlantic Ocean

Mexico

Five states border West Virginia.

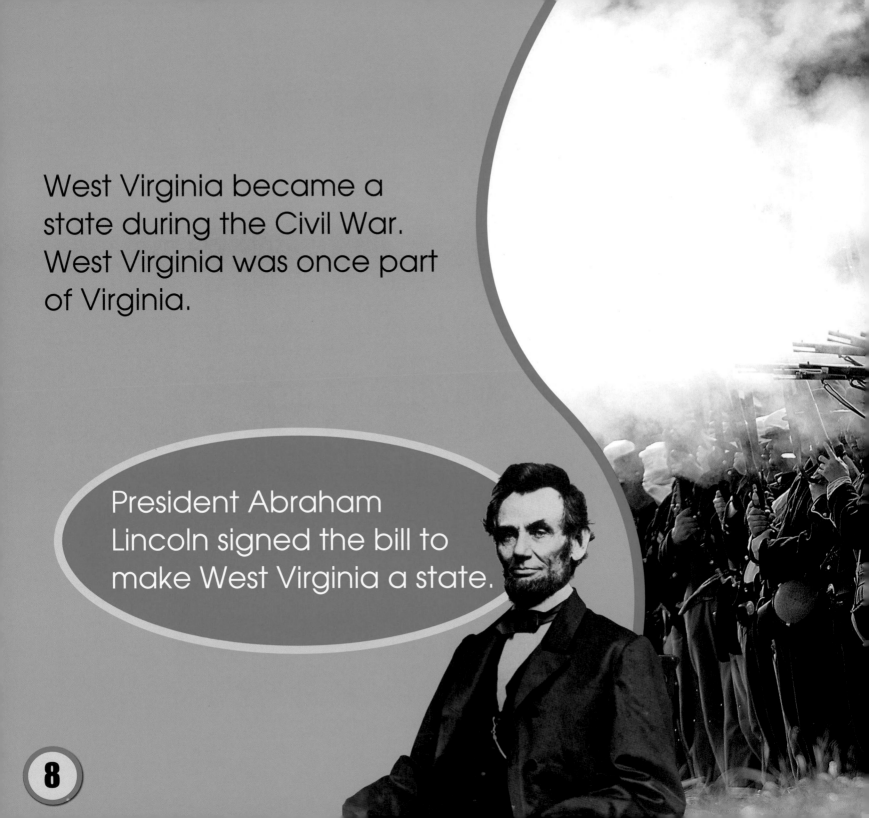

West Virginia became a state during the Civil War. West Virginia was once part of Virginia.

President Abraham Lincoln signed the bill to make West Virginia a state.

The rhododendron is the state flower of West Virginia. The name rhododendron means "rose tree."

The state seal has a farmer, a rock, and a miner.

Two rifles and a hat sit at the bottom of the seal.

This is the state flag of West Virginia. It shows the same picture as the state seal.

The rock has the date West Virginia became a state.

13

The black bear is the West Virginia state animal. Black bears can climb trees. They rest in dens in the winter.

Black bears are the only kind of bear that live in West Virginia.

This is the biggest city in West Virginia. It is named Charleston. It is the state capital.

Many boats come to Charleston on two big rivers in the city.

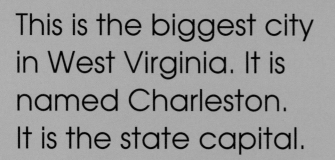

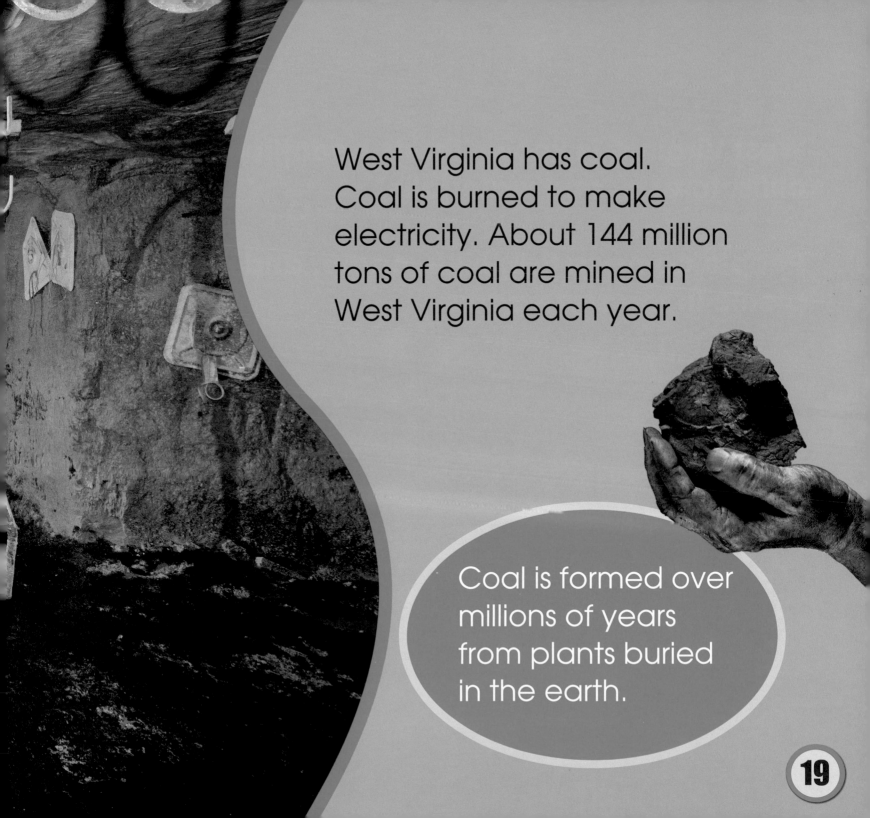

West Virginia has coal. Coal is burned to make electricity. About 144 million tons of coal are mined in West Virginia each year.

Coal is formed over millions of years from plants buried in the earth.

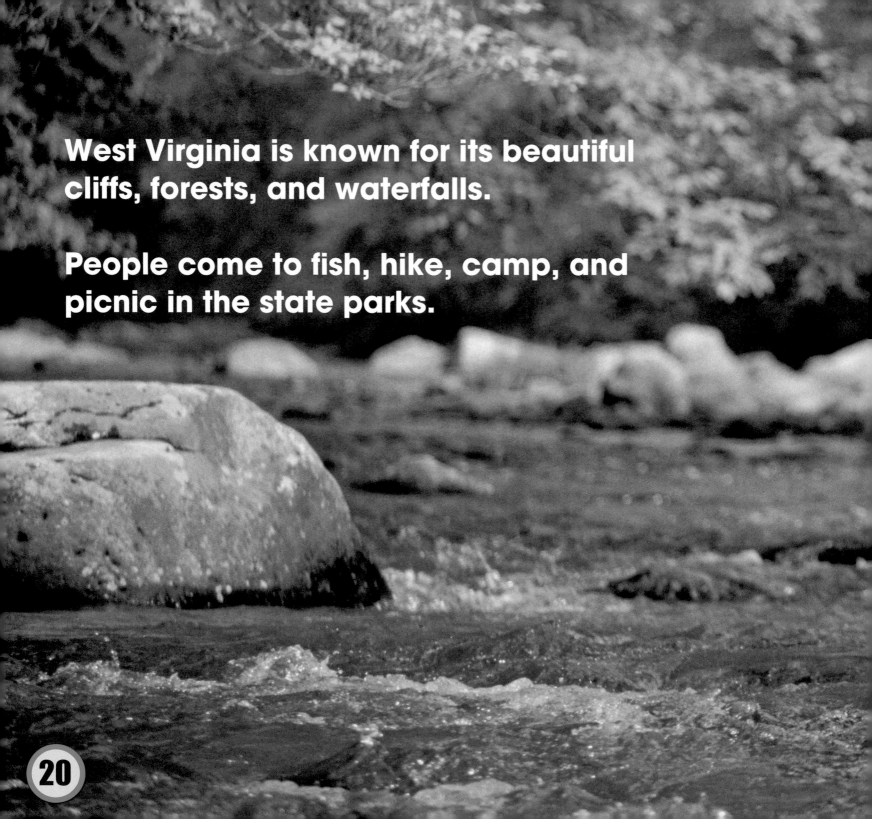

West Virginia is known for its beautiful cliffs, forests, and waterfalls.

People come to fish, hike, camp, and picnic in the state parks.

WEST VIRGINIA FACTS

These pages provide detailed information that expands on the interesting facts found in the book. These pages are intended to be used by adults as a learning support to help young readers round out their knowledge of each state in the *Explore the U.S.A.* series.

Pages 4–5

West Virginia is located in the Appalachian Mountain system. The Allegheny and Blue Ridge Mountain ranges are part of the Appalachian system. Most of the state is covered in rugged terrain. The flattest areas are found along West Virginia's rivers.

Pages 6–7

On June 20, 1863, West Virginia became the 35th state to join the United States. West Virginia is in the east central region of the United States. It is bordered by Ohio, Pennsylvania, Maryland, Virginia, and Kentucky. Two narrow pieces of land jut into other states. These are called panhandles. One lies between Pennsylvania and Ohio, and the other between Maryland and Virginia.

Pages 8–9

Virginia and West Virginia used to be one state. People on two sides of Virginia's mountains had different ideas about taxation and government. West Virginia separated from the Union in 1861 during the Civil War. The bill for West Virginia's statehood was approved by President Lincoln on January 1, 1863.

Pages 10–11

The state seal was adopted in 1863. Corn and a wheat sheaf stand behind the farmer. Barrels and an anvil sit behind the miner. In front of the rock are two rifles with a hat, known as a "liberty cap," resting on them. The cap represents the state and its willingness to defend its freedom.

Pages 12–13

The flag of West Virginia has the state coat of arms on a white background with a blue border. The state flower, the rhododendron, flanks the crest. The state motto is printed on the ribbon beneath the rifles. It is Latin and means "Mountaineers are always free."

Pages 14–15

Black bears can be many colors. They can be brown, cinnamon, white, beige, and even a shade of gray called "blue." Black bears are omnivores, which means they eat many different types of foods. A black bear's diet includes plants, insects, and animals. About 10,000 black bears live in West Virginia.

Pages 16–17

For many years, the state capital moved back and forth between Wheeling and Charleston. Based on a citizen vote, Charleston was named the state capital in 1885. Charleston lies where the Kanawha and Elk Rivers meet. The river valleys contain deposits of coal and natural gas.

Pages 18–19

Coal is the largest source of energy for making electricity in the world. It turns water into steam when it is heated. The steam is used to create electricity. More than 30,000 people work in West Virginia coal mines. There are 537 mines in the state. Coal makes the state about $3.5 billion each year.

Pages 20–21

West Virginia has more than 1.6 million acres (647,497 hectares) of state and national parkland, wildlife refuges, and forests. Cathedral State Park has ancient hemlock trees that grow up to 90 feet (27 meters) tall. Some are hundreds of years old. People visit parks and forests to hike, camp, fish, and boat.

KEY WORDS

Research has shown that as much as 65 percent of all written material published in English is made up of 300 words. These 300 words cannot be taught using pictures or learned by sounding them out. They must be recognized by sight. This book contains 52 common sight words to help young readers improve their reading fluency and comprehension. This book also teaches young readers several important content words, such as proper nouns. These words are paired with pictures to aid in learning and improve understanding.

Page	Sight Words First Appearance
5	is, it, made, many, mountain, of, state, the, this, up
7	in, part, where
8	a, make, once, to, was
11	and, at, has, means, name, tree, two
12	as, picture, same, shows
15	animal, are, can, kind, live, only, that, they
16	big, city, come, on, rivers
19	about, each, earth, from, over, plants, year
20	for, its, people

Page	Content Words First Appearance
5	West Virginia
7	shape, United States
8	Abraham Lincoln, bill, Civil War, president, Virginia
11	bottom, farmer, flower, hat, miner, rhododendron, rifles, rock, seal
12	date, flag
15	black bear, dens, winter
16	boats, capital, Charleston
19	coal, electricity, millions, tons
20	cliffs, forests, parks, waterfalls

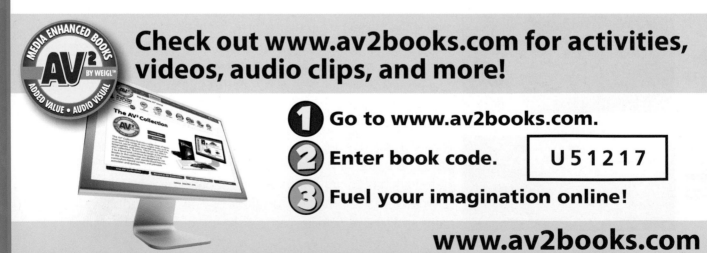

MEDIA ENHANCED BOOKS
AV² BY WEIGL™
ADDED VALUE · AUDIO VISUAL

Check out www.av2books.com for activities, videos, audio clips, and more!

The AV² Collection

1 Go to www.av2books.com.

2 Enter book code. | U 5 1 2 1 7 |

3 Fuel your imagination online!

www.av2books.com